DAPHNE

Illuminated by a daring and brilliant "alphabetical light," *Daphne* by Kristen Case reveals "tree-life" as a "shivering and light-saturated language," one where "possibilities of leaf-light are layered into a picture of infinity." Dazzlingly erudite and intimately lyrical, Case's poems embody a philosophy of desire within the embrace of the human imagination, one where the poet reconfigures trauma and memory. Daphne also explores the artistic realm of ekphrasis in an astute reading of Bernini's statue of Daphne and Apollo while engaging in thoughtful dialogue with sister poems like "Ode on a Grecian Urn" by Keats: "Beauty is truth, truth beauty." Offering notes on classical aesthetics interwoven with gorgeous seaweed wrack "inking" the Maine coast, this tree-lined book of laurels offers the radiant, mythological transformations of our daily lives: "In the moment love is consumed by its machinery, personhood slips out and seals itself in wood."

—Karen An-hwei Lee,
author of *The Beautiful Immunity* and *Phyla of Joy*

What does tradition afford the figure eclipsed or possessed by its foundational gestures? Drawing on sources as diverse as the haunting myth of Daphne and Apollo and Ludwig Wittgenstein's *On Certainty*, Kristen Case engages the Western tradition to examine the way violence disrupts and yet paradoxically unleashes understanding, illuminating the ways that knowledge is inextricably tied to experiences of both beauty and brutality. The recurring refrain from Wittgenstein's lover, "I long to be with you in any open space," serves as a poignant motif throughout the collection's brave yearning for connection that transcends predatory impulses. Daphne's tonic utterances make way for such an opening.

—Karla Kelsey

A refrain piercingly thrills its way throughout the entirety of Kristen Case's newest collection, "I long to be with you in any open space," though she didn't write those words herself. Their source is a letter from Francis Skinner, lover of Ludwig Wittgenstein, the philosopher who feared that an erotic life forsook a truthful one. That plaintive sentence returns us over and again to the touchstone cares of Daphne's crisis: Eros and Void, longing and open space. I mean simply to suggest that Kristen Case is at work in a kind of first-philosophy, which is now as it has always been, also a first-poetry, and the primary tenets of her concern are the very mythological fundaments that occupied Hesiod, Parmenides, and Empedocles. Case reminds us, as a genuine poet must, that we have yet to resolve the oppositions of our nature: mind and body, soul and thing, voice and void. In doing so, she traces lyric's ravished eons in which violence and love bewilderingly interpenetrate, from Daphne and Apollo, to Keats and the Grecian Urn. How intimate thought is in the body that holds the thinking, how intricate the voice that sings of woundedness out the wound that is the mouth. In essays that wild into lyric, in lyrics that assay her own experience, we find a book skeptical of the traditions it also believes in, such is the crux of being in the penetralium, where eros is also epistemology.

—Dan Beachy-Quick

Recent and Selected titles from Tupelo Press

Nebulous Vertigo Belle Ling
Westminster West Chard de Niord
Jalousie Allyson Paty
Mycocosmic Lesley Wheeler
Phantom Number: An Abecedarium for April Spring Ulmer
The Last Milkweed Alan Berolzheimer, Jeffrey Levine, & Allison O'Keefe, eds.
The Haunting Cate Peebles
The Radiant Lise Goett
The Opening Ritual G.C. Waldrep
Called Back Rosa Lane
Landsickness Leigh Lucas
The Right Hand Christina Pugh
Green Island Liz Countryman
The Beautiful Immunity Karen An-hwei lee
Small Altars Justin Gardiner
Country Songs for Alice Emma Binder
Asterism Ae Hee Lee
then telling be the antidote Xiao Yue Shan
Therapon Bruce Bond & Dan Beachy-Quick
membery Preeti Kaur Rajpal
How To Live Kelle Groom
Sleep Tight Satellite Carol Guess
THINE Kate Partridge
The Future Will Call You Something Else Natasha Sajé
Night Logic Matthew Gellman
The Unreal City Mike Lala
Wind—Mountain—Oak: Poems of Sappho Dan Beachy-Quick
Tender Machines J. Mae Barizo
Best of Tupelo Quarterly Kristina Marie Darling, Ed.
We Are Changed to Deer at the Broken Place Kelly Weber
Why Misread a Cloud Emily Carlson
The Strings Are Lightning and Hold You In Chee Brossy
Ore Choir: The Lava on Iceland Katy Didden and Kevin Tsang
The Air in the Air Behind It Brandon Rushton

DAPHNE

Kristen Case

Tupelo Press
North Adams, MA

Daphne

ISBN: 978-1-961209-20-6 (paperback)

Library of Congress Control Number: 2025932623
Cataloging-in-Publication data available on request.

Cover and text designed by Allison O'Keefe.

First paperback edition June 2025

Thank you to the editors of the following journals, in which some of these poems have previously appeared:

"Tonic 3 (Daphne)" and "Tonic 4 (Thoreau)" were first published in
The Cafe Review.
"O (After Hamlet)" appeared in *The Maine Review*.
"On Certainty" appeared in *Carolina Quarterly Review* and *Middlelost*.
"Daphne" appeared in *Beloit Poetry Review*.

Tupelo Press
P.O. Box 1767
North Adams, Massachusetts 01247
(413) 664-9611 / Fax: (413) 664-9711
editor@tupelopress.org / www.tupelopress.org

Tupelo Press is an award-winning independent literary press that publishes fine fiction, non-fiction, and poetry in books that are a joy to hold as well as read. Tupelo Press is a registered 501(c)(3) non-profit organization, and we rely on public support to carry out our mission of publishing extraordinary work that may be outside the realm of the large commercial publishers. Financial donations are welcome and are tax deductible.

CONTENTS

"Whoso List to Hunt"	1
Hind	3
Daphne	5
Tonic	17
On Certainty	18
Tonic	40
Horror Vacui	41
Tonic	48
Unravish'd	49
Tonic	63
Plenum	64
Six Variations on Beethoven's Opus 109	65
Night Sea	74
Early / Often	76
O	77
Tonic	80
Late Spring	81
Arks of Reprieve	82
Ritual	83
Plenum with Void	84
The Invisible Country of Remade Desire	85
Notes	87

Whoso list to hunt, I know where is an hind,
But as for me, *hélas*, I may no more.
The vain travail hath wearied me so sore,
I am of them that farthest cometh behind.
Yet may I by no means my wearied mind
Draw from the deer, but as she fleeth afore
Fainting I follow. I leave off therefore,
Sithens in a net I seek to hold the wind.
Who list her hunt, I put him out of doubt,
As well as I may spend his time in vain.
And graven with diamonds in letters plain
There is written, her fair neck round about:
Noli me tangere, for Caesar's I am,
And wild for to hold, though I seem tame.

—Thomas Wyatt

HIND (after Thomas Wyatt's "Whoso List to Hunt")

"Whoso List to Hunt" wrests the sonnet from Petrarch's Italian into English. It is made of hunger.

Picture an animal moving through bright leaves. You like to hunt? Wyatt asks. He is a hunter speaking to hunters.

Just before the turn at the end of line eight, the hunter's breath gives out, becomes general: wind from a net.

The sestet repeats the octave's opening line but with a difference: the generalized infinitive *to hunt* is particularized via an object: You want to hunt *her*?

Though his body fails, the poet may not withdraw his mind from the deer, his captor. This is his travail—the way the mind bolts from the exhausted body, tugging at its leash.

Fainting I follow marks a metrical disruption, a dactyl followed by a troche, five syllables of what is sometimes called "falling meter." This is where he falls.

Travail comes from medieval Latin, *trepalium*, meaning "three stakes" and referring to an instrument of torture.

In the sestet, the poet imagines his replacement, another hunter whose time will be spilled out like breath or like semen. The sonnet makes an economy of these expenditures.

Graven draws writing back to the kill, which is, though the beauty of the poem almost lets us forget it, the object of this hunt.

Noli me tangere—touch me not—is from Pliny the Elder, who describes deer wearing the inscription around their necks 300 years after Caesar's death. In the gospel of John, it is what Jesus says to Mary Magdalene after he rises from the tomb. In both cases, linked to deathlessness.

The voice of the hind is not a voice at all but a collar decorated with an *I*, a circular form in which total possession becomes a wildness and wildness a form of possession.

The last lines have eleven and nine syllables respectively, and so seem unsteady in the context of the poem's overall ten syllable line pattern. I imagine this unsteadiness as the holy ghost of an actual animal.

The hind is barely there at all, only a *fair neck*. Anybody's. You like to hunt?

Sometimes a slight constriction of the throat. You can't take it off.

DAPHNE

1.

Translucence of backlit maple leaf, dappled radiance of half-shaded maple leaf, cool heaviness of clustered and all-shadowed maple leaf. O infinite, O alphabet of sun-in-leaves. Numberless run of the singular. Numberless run of the multiple multiplied. O flashing current all through.

Let us consider her: a girl become, by the force of her own prayer, hard and silent and arboreal.

Among other things, the Daphne/Apollo myth is an etiology: the story of how Apollo became linked to the laurel tree. In some versions, it is also the story of how Apollo became a poet: like Orpheus's song, Apollo's art is given in consolation for the loss that initiates it.

The story goes like this: a girl/woman is chased after and lost. She becomes a lost thing. The man becomes a poet. In my early readings of the various iterations of this story, I imagined myself a chaser.

2.

On a morning in late May I find myself sitting in a small, six-sided room in a museum in front of a painting by Agnes Martin, thinking about the meanings of capture and escape, and whether one can capture or escape those meanings, or what beauty might be if it were not experienced inside a story of capture and escape.

A critic: *It is dramatically satisfying that rape and violence should occur at the ultimate place of refuge: in the dark recesses of the woods, where the heat of the sun is excluded, in a virginal setting, in those very woods where Diana herself maintains her realm as the defender of virginity.*

How may these threads be separated? The god, the girl fleeing, the prayer, the tree, the crown, the critic's dramatic satisfactions.

Her language sounds, perhaps, the way Martin's "Night Sea" would sound if a painting could sound. A small electric thing repeated, each time the same, each time minutely different, the hand becoming evident when you come close, a breathing irregularity held inside the grid of the regular, a fluttering, a pulse coming through it. When you stand close to the painting you can see how this electricity is created, is ongoingly created, by the small movements of a human hand, by overlapping and minutely different shades of blue paint, by quivering lines which are in fact tiny gaps between the blue rectangles.

3.

When I first made a grid I happened to be thinking of the innocence of trees and then this grid came into my mind and I thought it represented innocence, and I still do.

In Ovid the lost virgin girls, Daphne, Syrinx, and Arethusa, mean: the space between what is wanted and what may be had.

The stories are told in different voices but contain many of the same elements: the girl is a servant to Diana, goddess of the hunt. She scorns marriage, is careless of her hair, desires to remain a virgin. Hunted by a god, she prays for deliverance. At the moment of her capture she becomes: a laurel tree, a stream, a weeping cloud, a spring.

A critic: *The end of the hunt regularly is an actual or ritual death.*

In the instant before transformation, both Daphne and Arethusa feel their pursuer's breath on their hair. This detail is picked up in Pope's version of the Syrinx story in *Windsor Forest.*

And now his shorter breath, with sultry air,
Pants on her neck, and fans her parting hair.

4.

In American Sign Language the sign for "applause" is shaking two hands in the air. The sign for "hearing applause," according to the online ASL guide I consulted, is to *mimic clapping*.

Movement of little waves on the water, movement of leaves. Shudder of bright, shudder of leaf light. Weightless, without a body, it comes to you through the shifting body of leaves.

Little leaf, little light. A movement you would not call *pleasure*.

I am thinking of the difference between clapping and mimicking clapping, the space occupied by that difference.

Imagine the sudden unfolding of leaves. A living rustle of light on water.

Is Daphne a suicide? It seems a poverty to think so.

In her film about Keats and Fanny Brawne, Jane Campion invents for Fanny a poesies of clothes, the intricate folds of a ruffled collar flashing like leaves around her throat.

5.

Two possibilities:

1. We could imagine Daphne's tree-life as a sort of freedom. For this version, the only part of the story we change is her silence. In its place: a shivering and light-saturated language, silent only to the inattentive, and a resistance so entire that it grows past what it resists and becomes something wholly beyond the grammar of capture.

   Or,

2. we could imagine the scene without the hunt. What if the laurel crown were not a consolation? What if the runners ran together toward some beckoning ecstasy? What if Apollo felt not grief but joy at Daphne's strange and sudden flourishing?

The second version is harder to believe.

6.

When I was [ ] a man twice [ ] known [
] child. He [ ] and expertly [
][ ] couldn't move until [
] weeping cloud. [
] (the lifting? unbutton-[ ] I cannot [
][
] then frozen and insens[
] ongoing and [ ] movement of [
] *happeningness* of [ ]. I
recall a *no* [ ] did not speak itself in the absence
of any question, [ ] lifted and
handled [ ].

But there was a question.

It was: "fast or slow?" These being the options I said, "fast."

This presence of this element of choice made this occasion into a kind of flickering short circuit at the far end of my memory: I could speak, I could not speak. Consenting subject, inert object.

I am interested in the relation between my becoming frozen and insensible and Daphne's becoming arboreal, the way both occur at the moment of being caught. The trauma literature calls this response "tonic immobility" *an evolutionary adaptive defense to an attack by a predator when other forms of defense are not possible.* The trauma literature also says this response may exacerbate psychic harm in the aftermath of the event: feelings of shame and worthlessness, etc.

Tonic immobility is sometimes called *thanatosis* or "apparent death." Though the trauma literature suggests that this state is detrimental to assault victims, preventing them from effectively resisting, I am compelled by the implications of the word "tonic," which as an adjective can mean both restoring or preserving of heath and relating to the home key in tonal music. I want to imagine that the immobilized body holds some evolutionary secret, that a body subject to tonic immobility might break or be broken into a new kind of singing.

An actual or a ritual death.

Sometimes a kind of blankness settles in and it is difficult to locate the substrate of ordinary beauty and pleasure that pull one toward, say, a better sentence. I am trying to reconceive of this blankness as a kind of quiet music. A tone. I am trying to imagine it as *tonic.*

A grid. *A drowsy numbness.*

The laurel is known for its uses in cooking (the aromatic bay leaf comes from the laurel tree) and it's medicinal properties, especially its use as a *salve for open wounds.*

One of my questions is about how much we have to give up. In "Ode on a Grecian Urn," the poem that for me most perfectly communicates the infinite as a lived idea, Keats describes the urn as a *still unravished bride.* The verb *to ravish* may mean: 1. To seize and carry off, 2. To rape, 3. To fill with intense delight.

What am I to do with this language?

For a long time I have been asking, is our delight recoverable?

7.

As a result of one of these stories or all of them I think often about the space between desire and love, and whether there is a space, and whether love is a laurel crown or a transformation past all capture or joy at another's strange and sudden flourishing, and whether desire is compatible with love or love's destroying machine.

I am always looking for proof that what looks like love is only the machinery of a desire which would kill its object and I am always finding it.

In the moment love is consumed by its machinery, personhood slips out and seals itself in wood.

One of my questions is about how much I have to give up.

8.

A weeping cloud distributes itself. A weeping cloud is a disbursal of small blue currents of equal size in all directions. A weeping cloud sheds so much feeling feeling ceases to feel anything beyond the labor of release and the labor of reception. Weeping, like shaking, is the body gone into ungatherable being.

Or now the shaking of this willow in the slight and continuous breeze within what might be collected as the porousness of a shared silence, or non-silence—the wind making little waves of light and sound through the languorous branches. This cicada.

9.

This morning there is rain in the trees, layers of rainsound on layers of leaf, a surround of it.

In the surround of rainsound, each nameless, shudder of wishing.

I am thinking of Oppen's *Of Being Numerous* and of the hermit thrush and of the sign for hearing applause.

What I am trying to describe is a world without any words on it.

The song of hermit thrush seems to come from many directions at once. It throws itself beyond itself.

When the singular is merged into an uncountable multitude of minute differences another kind of being is suggested. Suggests itself.
I want to suggest.

A laurel tree, a spring, a weeping cloud, a stream.

What tone, what tonic, what wordless repair?

TONIC 1

Imagine a place

you might

call *open space*

or *infinite* or

grid. Imagine an undifferent-

iated self

among selves, a canopy

through which light

moves, not a mass

but an intimacy dis-

persed. Imagine the

deepest possible sleep,

a solidarity of

longing.

ON CERTAINTY

If this be error and upon me prov'd;
I never writ, nor no man ever lov'd.

1.

Mornings I think about Rosemarie Waldrop's sentence *All resonance grows from consent to emptiness* and imagine a wordless being. The leaves move individually, slightly, and though their movement is independent of the light it changes the appearance of the light, which becomes watery. The leaves are lit, or half-lit, or shaded. These possibilities of leaf-light are layered into a picture of infinity.

I am reading Wittgenstein's *On Certainty*, his last work, posthumously assembled, in an old paperback edition that belonged to a now-dead poet who once lived in my town.

Consent to emptiness may be either the description of a progress or the description of a position. *This* suggests the near-to-hand. A hand is briefly near the word for it, then vanishes. In June, externally lit objects exceed their names and I begin various programs of self-regulation.

At dinner with an older couple who generally seem touchingly fond of each other I catch the man looking at the woman with contempt. It passes quickly, but it is all I remember about the evening.

In another book, Wittgenstein says this about pain: *Suppose everyone has a box with something in it: we call it a "beetle". No one can look into anyone else's box, and everyone says he knows what a beetle is only by looking at his beetle.*

I imagine the holder of the beetle box feeling a mixture of tenderness and revulsion toward the object inside. I wonder if the box is serving mainly to hide the beetle or to contain it. I wonder if Wittgenstein considered about other possible names for the thing in the box, like "rock" or "mouse," and whether these variations would change my impression of Wittgenstein's theory of pain.

The thing in the box, he says, *has no place in the language game at all.*

My initial, instinctive response to the man's contempt was to wonder why the woman has not learned, after so many years, how to avoid exposing herself to it.

Wittgenstein's *On Certainty* was translated by G.E.M. Anscombe, whose own work addresses, among other subjects, the difference between cognitive and conative states. The main difference is that a conative state involves desire.

According to his biographer, Ray Monk, Wittgenstein was highly influenced by a book he read as an adolescent called *Sex and Character* by Otto Weinenger.

Weinenger: *Women have no existence and no essence; they are not, they are nothing. Mankind occurs as male or female, as something or nothing. Woman has no share in ontological reality, no relation to the thing-in-itself, which in the deepest interpretation is the absolute, is God.*

Weinenger: *Woman is neither high-minded or low-minded, strong-minded or weak-minded. She is the opposite of all of these. Mind cannot be predicated of her at all; she is mindless.*

Weinenger: *Man is form; woman is matter.*

Weinenger also believed in a strict separation between love (masculine) and desire (feminine). Monk ascribes Wittgenstein's *conviction that sexuality is incompatible with the honesty that genius demands* to Weinenger's influence.

On Certainty: For months I have lived at address A, I have read the name of the street and the number of the house countless times, have received countless letters here and given countless people the address. If I am wrong about it, the mistake is hardly less that if I were (wrongly) to believe I was writing Chinese and not German.

I "know" but do not summon to clarity the negative adjectives you would use, internally, to describe me. My feeling of knowing that you use these words to yourself is like my feeling of knowing that my body has never been far from the surface of the earth. I feel close to them. If I were to pronounce these words inwardly it would be difficult not to imagine that we were in some way communicating.

If my friend were to imagine one day that he had been living for a long time in such and such a place etc. etc. I should not call this a mistake, *but rather a mental disturbance, perhaps a transient one.*

Wittgenstein imagines a friend who imagines a life of some duration about which he (Wittgenstein) gives us no details but suggests that such details (*such and such a place etc. etc.*) exist within the frame of the *mental disturbance*. I am interested in whether Wittgenstein was thinking of a particular friend when he wrote these sentences, at the end of his life, in response to a book by the philosopher G.E. Moore, who was his friend.

I am interested in the fact that Wittgenstein's translator was a woman. I google "Wittgenstein and women." The results are predictably disheartening.

Not every false belief of this sort is a mistake.

Even imaginary or failed intimacy entails a good deal of empirical knowledge.

The world of your thinking and feeling that I have built is like a miniature glass house, with glass furniture and glass appliances and glass boxes of cereal. It is hard not to feel tenderness towards this world even as I suspect that I have been all wrong about it. Or, rather, that it has been all wrong.

Wittgenstein also designed a house. You can see pictures of it online.

But what is the difference between a mistake and a mental disturbance? Or what is the difference between my treating it as a mistake and my treating it as a mental disturbance?

Before he died my father's particular delusions, which concerned the rules of baseball, the operations of clocks, and international terrorism, wove themselves together into a cohesive fabric, *a picture of the world*.

Can we say: a mistake *doesn't only have a cause, it also has a ground? i.e. roughly: when someone makes a mistake, this can be fitted into what he knows aright?*

I am wondering whether the ways I have been wrong about your thinking and feeling are more like being wrong about my address or being wrong about language. Or is it incorrect to say "wrong" in this context because the thinking and feeling of others is always a boxed beetle and not something it is possible to be right or wrong about? Was my mistake to believe in the possibility of mistakes (and therefore, of a ground of non-mistaking?)

Realizing that you have been wrong about another person's thinking or feeling is perhaps like realizing that you have made a mistake about your address, in spite of having received countless letters there. In this way it is also like a mental disturbance.

I am trying to write this *you* in a way that might point to any number of relations or lost relations but that is at the same time highly specific. I am trying to get at the specific way of being of this kind of mistake. I am not certain why I want to do this, what is at stake for me in this conative state.

I did not get my picture of the world by satisfying myself of its correctness; nor do I have it because I am satisfied of its correctness. No: it is the inherited background against which I distinguish between true and false.

My body resists paying attention to the knowledge I am trying to articulate and, in articulating, register: that the glass house I have been making is not *accurate*. Or perhaps, is not *habitable*. In the face of this knowledge I order new sheets and rearrange the objects of an actual house.

When a relation has moved into the inherited background, our wrongness about it becomes more consequential. The air is hot and full of dandelion seeds which drift like airy flakes across the deck and into the woods. The spiders' webs are full of them, dusty galaxies between the propane tanks, across the corners of flower boxes. It is difficult even to imagine a non-conative state. What size desert would I have to cross? how many days would it take?

What I want is not to be wrong in this particular way again.

2.

Time settles into everything. The hard seed is almost invisible, a grain between your fingers, the loose fibers make a cloud around it.

In the biography, Monk describes "personal remarks" that Wittgenstein left in code in his philosophical manuscripts.

The wet ends of the white towels I have hung on the clothesline fold on themselves in the grass, the towels' weight tugging the line groundward. Because they look so defeated, I consider repositioning the wooden clothespins at the ends of the line, shifting the towels away from the slack center where they are clustered, but am daunted by the energy this will require.

According to Monk, *these remarks were separated by Wittgenstein from his philosophical remarks by a simple code that he had learnt as a child (whereby a=z, b=y, c=x etc.).*

The grass is thick under the line: their contact with the ground is unlikely to make the towels dirty. On the other hand, to admit this poverty of motivation seems dangerous, a threat to the whole infrastructure of my life.

When we first begin to believe anything, what we believe is not a single proposition, it is a whole system of propositions. (Light dawns gradually over the whole.)

I am particularly interested in the fact that these coded remarks exist side-by-side with Wittgenstein's philosophical writings, not in a separate notebook.

The wet ends of the white towels meet the grass in oblong shadow shapes.

What the coded remarks also reveal is the extraordinary extent to which Wittgenstein's love life and his sexual life went on only in his imagination.

Picture two elaborate glass structures, in some places connected by many small points to our actual lives and so, indirectly, to each other; in other places, split off entirely from the actual, built precariously out over the air.

Wittgenstein's perception of a relationship would often bear no relation at all to the perception of it held by the other person.

Or: one elaborate glass structure, and one person not imagining anything at all.

Gradually over the hole.

3.

From the translator's introduction to *On Certainty*: *The material falls into four parts... What we believe to be the first part was written on twenty loose sheets of lined foolscap, undated. These Wittgenstein left in his room in G.E.M. Anscombe's house in Oxford where he lived (apart from a visit to Norway in the Autumn) from April 1950 to February 1951.*

I try to picture G.E.M. Anscombe's house, and Wittgenstein's room in it. I think about what it means to have a room in someone else's house.

Anscombe: *I am under the impression that he wrote them in Vienna, where he had stayed from the previous Christmas until March, but I cannot recall now the basis of this impression.*

I try to picture the twenty loose sheets. When I zoom in to make it bigger, the text in front of my eyes blurs slightly for a half second and then refocuses as if to remind me that what I am writing is only an image of words, a photograph of words. A little string of ghosts.

I cannot recall the basis of my impression that certain men believe without articulating it to themselves that *mind cannot be predicated of me at all.*

The potted basil flourishes. I practice writing the word *beetle* using Wittgenstein's code.

The rest is in small notebooks, containing dates; toward the end, indeed, the date of writing is always given. The last entry is two days before his death on April 29 1951. We have left the dates exactly as they appear in the manuscripts.

I wonder whether Anscombe wrote the words of the introduction in a cognitive or a conative state.

Sunlight streaks the deck, the lilac, my daughter's easel, the spiders' webs between objects. Waking early you can see the way the night hangs on, and the way light penetrates at the threshold of visibility. The *you* I was writing has vanished, leaving only the diffuse and impersonal world.

4.

May 4:
[Here there is still a big gap in my thinking. And I doubt whether it will be filled now.]

Here there are gaps between sounds and between branches, a receding and a yawning forward of a dark between. I had sunk myself so deep into the wordless interior that when you failed to register the reflecting surround the shadows came for their objects and my name fell right off my face.

Violence is a secret key. Emptiness and the terror that attends it.

I spend the morning reading all the pages of the biography that relate to Wittgenstein's lover, Francis Skinner.

Outside one of the hemlocks is bare as though stripped, except for a few sparse branches at the top, its skeletal branches orient toward me as though reaching out while trying not to appear not to be reaching out, or like the tributaries of rivers on a map.

Skinner's letters were kept by Wittgenstein, and were found among his possessions after his death, and from them we can reconstruct how the relationship developed. (Wittgenstein's letters to Skinner were retrieved by Wittgenstein after Skinners death and were, presumably, burnt.)

In *On Certainty* Wittgenstein attempts, repeatedly, to illustrate that it is a false move in the language-game to say that you "know" or "believe" something that it is impossible for you to doubt. What we call "knowing" or "believing" bears a particular relationship to doubtfeeling.

(He is at pains, however, to remind us that our inability to doubt something does not necessarily make it true: *Certainty is as it were a tone of voice in which one declares how things are, but one does not infer from the tone of voice that one is justified.*)

I am interested in the untrue thing whose truth you can't doubt; in ways of being wrong that cannot be detached from the foundation of the language game and thus suggest that you might be wrong about the fabric of being.

It is nonsensical to say that I might be wrong about the fabric of being, but that is what I mean.

Francis to Wittgenstein: *I think a lot about our relation. Are we going to act independently of each other, will I be able to act independently of you?*

Wittgenstein, in coded remarks: *Lay with [Francis] two or three times. Always with the feeling there was nothing wrong in it, then with shame. Have also been unjust, edgy and insincere with him, and also cruel.*

I am trying to get closer to the feeling of abjection in its relation to conative states. This has something to do with the question of what is possible between people. What is possible between people has to do with the fabric of being I may be right or wrong about and also has to do with politics. After the rain the darkest-shadowed green in the layers of shadowed and half-shadowed leaves out my studio window is nearly black and hurtles through the generalized months into my particular mouth.

I return to the repeated *also* in the coded remarks about Francis. *Have also been unjust. Also cruel.* Monk calls him *Francis* rather than Skinner, though he mostly uses last names to refer to Wittgenstein, his colleagues, and his students. Probably there is a non-conative explanation but I imagine this as a slip that suggests a feeling of tenderness on the part of the biographer to the object of Wittgenstein's simultaneous desire and aversion, an unregistered and, in any case, totally unrealizable wish to console.

Monk: *What is striking is the juxtaposition of his account of their lying together with observations of his lovelessness toward Francis. Or perhaps what he is expressing is his fear of becoming loveless.*

In 1938 Wittgenstein translated, with a student named Yorick Smythies, portions of the mystic play *Raja* (often titled in English *King of the Dark Chamber*) by Rabindranath Tagore. The king to whom the title refers is never seen by anyone. According to Monk, *the play concerns the awakening – or, one might say the humbling, the subjugation – of the King's wife.*

I make a sketch for a glass structure called Lovelessness enclosed in a second glass structure called Fear of Lovelessness. I look at photographs of Haus Wittgenstein online.

Coded remarks: *Thought: it would be good and right if he had died, and thereby taken my "folly" away.*

yvvgov yvvgov yvvgov
yvvgov yvvgov yvvgov

5.

Riding my bicycle back to my desk I notice the single meandering track in the dirt made by my bicycle earlier in the day. It is startling to be confronted with my past self in this way.

When I feel that another person's desire for me carries with it the secret wish that I were dead, is this a mistake or a mental disturbance? Whose?

In the glass house of Lovelessness there is a dark chamber.

I read art books, look at pictures of art, consider Francis.

The window in front of my desk is a glass grid of twenty-five squares, marked off by white wooden frames. Above this grid is half circle of glass divided into four sections, each divided again into three. Light penetrates the layers of leaves, then penetrates these surfaces. It is strange to remember that this occurs *sequentially*.

A numbness attends certain conative states. These are several occasions and the same occasion. A winnowing of shimmering difference into a single darkness, dispersion of sensation into the surround. The trunk and branches of the almost-dead hemlock are stark, lichen-marked. It has to do with the feeling of being wished dead.

Francis to Wittgenstein: *I feel very unhappy that I should have given you cause to write that you feel I'm away from you. It is a terrible thing that I have acted in a way that might loosen what is between us. It would be a catastrophe for me if anything happened to our relation. Please forgive me for what I have done.*

I know that it is likely a matter of translation but I am moved by the urgent simplicity of the phrase "I feel very unhappy." I can't imagine uttering this phrase. I can type it, however, with little feeling of self-consciousness: I am only depressing the small back squares on this mark-making machine.

I feel very unhappy.

Mornings you feel the little winter inside of August. In the trees a single hermit thrush bodies the air in sound, which penetrates as if to loosen what is between. I consult the weather of the future and check to see what my device has collected while I slept. Through the canopy, the early sunlight finds the trunks of two maples which radiate accordingly though the comparative gloom.

Wittgenstein retracts the wish that Francis *had died* in subsequent sentences. Though of course it may only be an accident of translation, I am interested in this strange grammatical formulation, as though Wittgenstein were conjuring not a single imaginary event but a whole imaginary world in which Francis *had died.*

Francis did, in fact, die—of polio—in 1941. By this time, the biography notes, the relationship *had deteriorated.*

The wanting-dead with which I am concerned, if real at all, is of course the unconscious kind which has to do with one's being a woman and not with one's personal qualities, or the personal qualities of the person or persons who may or may not unconsciously and surely only momentarily wish me dead.

I consider which of the following, if any, Wittgenstein would allow:

No one really wishes me dead.

I do not believe that anyone really wishes me dead.

I know no one really wishes me dead.

I may be mistaken, but I do not believe that anyone really wishes me dead.

When I am feeling very unhappy I turn to the pages in my art books with reproductions of paintings by Agnes Martin. In one of these, alternating dark and light gray stripes are overlaid with a grid of small rectangles, drawn in pencil, which creates the feeling of infinite repetition in all directions. This painting is called "The Tree." After looking at it for some time the sensation of being wished dead disperses into image, the book, the table, and the screened-in porch in which I am sitting.

The argument "I may be dreaming" is senseless for this reason: if I am dreaming, this remark is being dreamed as well—and indeed it is also being dreamed that these words have any meaning.

I touch the tiny black squares of the mark-making machine, which makes a clicking sound as if to remind me someone's home.

6.

I do not know how the sentence "I have a body" is to be used.

Saplings in the understory, mainly beech. Wide-leafed to the sun. Imagine a feeling like a grid. Like a canopy.

Francis, Monk writes, *is remembered by all who knew him as shy, unassuming, good-looking, and above all, extraordinarily gentle.*

The bicycle tracks multiply in the dirt. Unmoving, they mean *movement*. I move along them, tracking. The long coast downhill is a wordless impersonal pleasure, like a painting.

He was also *utterly, uncritically and almost obsessively devoted to Wittgenstein.*

In the sentence Wittgenstein doesn't know how to use, the *I* hovers above the syntax and its body, claiming possession. I want most to be dispossessed, released into a wordless and grid-like ether. I consider *The King in the Dark Chamber* and wonder if humbling and subjugation are necessary for this escape.

The feeling of being wished dead, like the feeling of being thought of as *matter*, is likely related to an event. The details of this event are so typical and uninteresting I am embarrassed to recount them. (He was twice my age; it seemed romantic and exciting at first; I froze but did not verbally refuse; he moved very quickly; afterwards I cried and walked home alone, etc.)

Light breaks and remakes itself in the almond-shaped beech leaves and the hand-shaped maple leaves and the tear-shaped birch leaves in the canopy, each with its gradually shifting portion of shadow and its gradually shifting portion of light. They make a reflection like water on the saplings beneath them. Even the striped-bare hemlock is beautiful.

All resonance grows from consent to emptiness.

Skinner to Wittgenstein, March 25, 1934: *I long to be with you in any open space.*

I repeat this sentence to myself in my mind, imagining any open space, imagining a desire so extraordinarily gentle. I wonder where Francis is buried. Last night's rain erased my bicycle tracks, so riding to the studio I have the sensation that time has started over.

I do not often think about the event but when I do I cannot shake my surprise that I have allowed something so banal to contort my interior life in this lasting way. I have no feelings at all about the person who lifted and handled my body as though it were a dead animal: why have I stored and reanimated, thousands of times, the view of myself and my body his treatment of me seemed to signal? In particular, why the feeling of valuelessness, of inert deadness, of being so much disposable matter?

I cannot be certain he knew anything at all about what I felt. The words we use for this kind of event depend on variables that are in this case, uncertain. It may have been a mistake.

I do not know how the sentence “I have a body” is to be used. Whose body? How it is to be used?

I long to be with you

in any open space.

TONIC 2

The striated or interstitial, any
thing (fern or oak leaf,
for instance) that is
made of its own
absence. Also the deep-
grooved body of the oak or the
immense calm of the near-
autumnal light
on the surface
of the blackened and lin-
eated stump. These squares
of lit stone, their gentle
indifference. Any
open.

HORROR VACUI

We can speak and think only of what exists. And what exists is uncreated and imperishable for it is whole and unchanging and complete. It was not or nor shall be different since it is now, all at once, one and continuous.
—Parmenides, *On Nature*

The old problem of the void is now wholly superseded by the problem of reference to the non-existent; the distinction has gradually been drawn between empty space with all of its subtle and complex properties and nothing, which, I will argue, has no properties at all.
—J.K. Swindler, "Parmenides' Paradox: Negative Reference and Negative Existentials"

The pyrrhic is rightfully dismissed. Its existence in either ancient or modern rhythm is purely chimerical, and the insisting on so perplexing a nonentity as a foot of two short syllables, affords, perhaps, the best evidence of the gross irrationality and subservience to authority which characterise our Prosody.
—Edgar Allan Poe, "The Rationale of Verse"

That's a fair thought to lie between maids' legs.
—Shakespeare, *Hamlet*

1.

Empty space with all its complex and subtle properties flowers in the dark month. A difference in invisibles multiplies—a gray-blue dawn; dawning gray-blue; gray-blue in the dawn.

A spatial void would require an idiom.

The snow begins its steady disappearance, little pockets of air in the lace, a crystalline.

Wholly superseded you show an understandable tendency, a low purple light, a portion of internal air.

But no properties. No properties at all.

2.

For among these Februaries is one so endlessly February that only by Februarying through it will your heart survive.

You begin to formulate a theory of nonfeeling as an interpersonal event.

On the bright concrete, one or two trees make a thicket of shadows. A list of forms that include emptiness would be a list all forms. A plenum of forms.

Nonfeeling as some thing that can be received and absorbed into the self as a positive absence, a discrete void.

For example, Eliot's "Portrait of a Lady." Her lilacs.

3.

The philosophical articles are full of warnings about the differences between nonbeing and the void.

(As a nonphilosopher I largely ignore these warnings.)

The feeling of non-being or void is distinct from the garbage feeling but closely related. The subject of my study is the transformation of one into the other.

The light is lighting things, successively. Certain distinctions present themselves.

One of the Februaries is called evening. You proceed on the premise of a regular forgetting. This vacancy lasts a given number of minutes, which can be arrested at the location desired. A midsized oblivion, infinitely repeatable.

In a book, you read about the almost unfathomable emptiness of atoms. On the internet, you read about famous misogynists.

4.

Consider violence as a movement between bodies: first inside to outside, then outside to inside.

If mood or feeling can be transferred between persons by means of, for example, infinitely repeatable sound sequences shared via text message, void may also be a kind of currency.

When you are not feeling the garbage feeling it is difficult to believe in it. Your atoms seem no emptier than anyone else's.

Globes of light along the gray-brown body of the lilac; lichens on the rain dark bodies of trees.

But it is true you often feel like a container. *Receptacle* is the word you think.

(Note: *void as a kind of currency.*)

5.

It is important to remember that there are degrees of void-transference. Once you are habituated to garbage feeling your system may default to it when exposed to mild, everyday instances.

Void-absorption has particular effects on the time-field. Each void episode weakens the seams.

In March the stream is running again, but hardened snow remains in the braches and among the cavities of the woodpile and along the black power lines. Shadows notable in the new light.

Able to be noted, worthy of notice, speakable. Tendrils of a houseplant graze the windowlight.

(Note: *Preserve a space in the form for void. A pyrrhic.*)

6.

The Ancient physicians were concerned with the operation of void in the body. For example, Erasistratus held that the circulation of bodily fluid was driven by the imperative to prevent the formation of a vacuum.

I think of Simone Weil thinking about the *Iliad* and starving herself. Her body. Her self.

In the *Timeaus*, Plato asserts the existence of a third kind of being, alongside forms and images of forms: *an invisible and formless being which receives all things and in some mysterious way partakes of the intelligible, and is most incomprehensible.* He calls this third kind, which is the amorphous stuff out of which the Craftsman makes the world, "the receptacle." Sometimes he calls it "the mother substance."

It is true that sometimes I seek confirmation of the garbage feeling. I put this down to a drive for, at the least, certainty.

7.

Any depiction of the void is of course a metaphor.

The garbage feeling may be accompanied by a particular kind of coldness, localized to the body. A kind of solipsistic weather.

In the "pre-cosmic" state (the state "prior to" the intervention of the Craftsman) the receptacle is subject to erratic and disorderly motions, and moves its contents in turn. Its contents are mere "traces."

Of all the things I could tell you, *what happened* explains the least.

Parmenides describes the universe as plenum: a kind of wall of being (his word is *eon*) with no cracks in it.

(Note:)

8.

Aristotle, too, believed void to be impossible because of the way matter keeps rushing in. He defines void as *a place with no thing in it.*

Goldfinches cluster near the plastic feeder, still in their winter feathers.

Dark pours out from the open barn doors into the greater dark. A layer of hard snow covers the yard and the visible roofs. Subject to erratic and disorderly motions, you practice shifting your address.

Weil: *To define force—it is that x that turns anybody who is subjected to it into a thing. Exercised to the limit, it turns man into a thing in the most literal sense: it makes a corpse out of him. Somebody was here, and the next minute there is nobody here at all.*

Outside the dark occupies things generally though some of the windows are lit. Space with all of its subtle and complex properties intercedes first between the broad dark branches of fir trees, then between the thin particular branches of maple trees. Of course this order is imaginary; in fact the subtle and complex properties are everywhere at once.

9.

Annihilating all that's made
To a green thought in a green shade.

(Note: *pyrrhic spondee pyrrhic spondee*)

10.

The transferability of nonfeeling suggests an occult relation. The emptiness of your atoms nods to the emptiness of mine.

In voidier moods, I browse the love letters and biographies of famous misogynists like a wolf circling a trap.

Eliot made it a rule that they could not dine together on consecutive nights.

I bookmark the one with the photograph of the letters and the lengthy statement of disavowal addressed to a distant future.

11.

Imagine Eliot saying, *EonEonEonEonEon* into the distant future, a wide trochaic wall.

Imagine a pyrrhic threat, beginning in your own atoms and leaking everywhere.

Imagine void had a touchable body. Imagine wanting to end it.

The typed envelopes are tied with a ribbon.

Imagine the nothing you would feel, untying it.

TONIC 3 (DAPHNE)

Proximate to the dark mossy under-

          story and the watery leaflight you

forget the sentences

          about your body and its capture

the words falling from you one

          by one even as you feel them

becoming: green and

          green and green and

the way light enters you and

          your whole being leaning toward

the thin and continual and indifferent exchange,

          a pale moss of repeated small forms over-

taking your skin, even this

          annihilation now a kind of harmony.

UNRAVISH'D

These hemlocks ice ensilvered, light encased. These beeches whose wheat-colored leaves alone are left, Decembered in the gray-green surround, to register the movement of invisible matter. White lichen on the bodies of these. Severally, singly, they shiver. Whitely dispersed, the light mutes the hum of a dark solidarity, delivers the long depth of the wood, everywhere its echo's slow-goldening insistence particularizes.

Keats says *Thou* to it, the urn, this artifact. Later he makes it speak.

Unravish'd calls ahead to the poet-speaker's accusation: *Cold Pastoral!* And, taken together with the questions that cascade down the end of the first stanza, establishes the urn as withholding, like the *maidens loth* who are the object of the *mad pursuit*.[1] That this withholding is at once sexual and epistemological is corollary to the commonplace idea of knowing as penetration. *Unravish'd bride* positions the urn, like the object of the *Bold Lover* in stanza two, as poised forever at the moment before certain possession, between wedding and consummation: Daphne in flight, her fingers already leafing, as in Bernini's statue.

---

1 It seems only right to acknowledge that none of this matters much to the poem, that *unravish'd bride* is only meant to gesture at the urn's uncanny and remarkable continuance, and that the whole system of meanings around *unravish'd*, including the understanding of feminine resistance as central to experiences of both male and female pleasure, hardly belongs exclusively to Keats—is a well-established trope in the Classical myth and poetry on which Keats drew, for example—and further, is not a primary focus of any of the dense networks of meanings and images that make up the poem. What follows is, in its focus on a more-or-less incidental element of the poem, an exercise in perversely intentional misreading intended as an act of love.

The poem's famous tonal ambivalence—its measured equivocations between the poles of *Cold Pastoral!* and *friend to man*—reflect its understanding of the ways frustration feeds imagination: it is *because* the urn withholds its answers about the sacrifice in stanza four that the poet-speaker's imagination can supply the *little town by river or sea shore, / Or mountain built with peaceful citadel / ...emptied of this folk, this pious morn*. This is, for Keats, the profounder penetration of imagination (as distinct from mere knowing) by the poet, who, as he writes in a letter to Richard Woodhouse, "has no Identity" but is "continually in for—and filling in some other Body." It is precisely by withholding the truth of its stories that the urn engages the poet-speaker to engender Truth upon it: its beauty teases out, *asks for*, this secondary possession by filling-in. In this way, the paradox of *unravish'd bride* is resolved: it is in not being possessed that she is joined with, filled in, by each generation in its turn.

Maybe my question is: how can I be a poet?

Or maybe it is: how can I be inside both the poem and my own body?

Thou eastlit frozen wood, thou shiver of hemlock, thou cloud of light.

In Bernini's statue, the rhyming of the two bodies, god and girl—her arched back echoing the curve of his torso, his downward trailing arm in line with her upward extended one, wind in both their hair—belies the opposition of their wills. Daphne's mouth is a small blank o. Opposition is folded into counterpoint, contrast within a scheme of harmony, all of it white upon white upon white, marbled, deepshadowed.

At the stream the black water tumbles under skeins of ice, clear at the edge and fingered, a constellation of rounded filaments fringed round its still moving source and opposition. Silent but for the water. Even the beech leaves are still.

My favorite writer on Keats reminds me that it is a funeral urn, designed to hold ashes. He says, "It is worth considering that the words Keats hears from the Urn's mouth are spoken out of that empty blank within it, that unrepresentable space the container contains." The urn holds, or is meant to hold, human remains. But Keats's identification of the urn as a bride reminds us that death is here is only the other face of erotic love, nuptial possession, procreative power. The urn is another penetralium, enclosed space, source of mysteries: blank in itself, holder of everything.

Of course it is a woman.

Now in the woods the January sunlight dazzles, makes the world a dazzlement, says that beauty is just this possession of the dark woodworld by light, this surfeit of brightness at the edge of the stream, this movement of air-light over the body of water-light held by light translucent, cold liquid light immobilized, fingering out into the shimmering dark.

Empty blank brings me close to what I want to think, which is nothing, or rather: a something being made a nothing, an annihilation. I am interested in the precise kind of annihilation that is effected by the act of rape, thought in terms of its place in a constellation of poetic ideas that are my own as much as they are anybody's. I am interested in the relation between this annihilation and the felt annihilation experienced by the actual (breathing human) subject, or perhaps I mean object, of actual (breathing human) violence. I am interested in this intersection of the external and the internal, the real and the imagined. Because rape has to do with volition and the nullification of volition, it necessarily has to do not only with bodies but also with the internal and invisible.

Ravish: 1.*To seize and carry off* 2.*To rape* 3.*To fill with intense delight*

Maybe I want, somewhat perversely, is to literalize the mythopoetic act of ravishment, to insist upon the actual.

Maybe what I want is to poeticize the merely and boringly brutal.

Beauty is truth, truth beauty.

In *The Iliad, or The Poem of Force* Simone Weil writes that force "is that *x* that turns anybody who is subjected to it into a thing. Exercised to the limit, it turns man into a thing in the most literal sense: it makes a corpse out of him. Somebody was here, and in the next moment there is nobody here at all."

Rape is of course different than murder. It does not turn the body into a corpse but rather takes possession of the body-as-thing, overriding or nullifying the other's interiority.

> From its first property (the ability to turn a human being into a thing by the simple method of killing him) flows another, quite prodigious too in its own way, the ability to turn a human being into a thing while he is still alive. He is alive; he has a soul; and yet—he is a thing. An extraordinary entity this—a thing that has a soul. And as for the soul, what an extraordinary house it finds itself in! Who can say what it costs it, moment by moment, to accommodate itself to this residence, how much writhing and bending, folding and pleating are required of it? It was not made to live inside a thing; if it does so, under pressure of necessity, there is not a single element of its nature to which violence is not done.

Today the stream is frozen over and covered except for a few dark pools. Underneath, it still sounds: a cold, breathing, a sunlit language. I make a path to it through the new snow. The angled light cuts and cuts and cuts where it will.

how much writhing and bending, folding and pleating

I have moved too quickly from subject to object: from the perspective of the poet-speaker who seeks to penetrate the withholding object to the perspective of the human-object whose body is subject to penetration.

Maybe this holding of two perspectives, or the rapid shuttling between them, is my problem. In a given moment of reading, I do not know whether to be the man-poet or the woman-urn.

I want to return to Keats's speaking *to* the object, his saying *Thou* to it.

> When *thou* is spoken, the speaker has no thing for his object. For where there is a thing there is another thing. Every *It* is bounded by others. *It* exists only by being bounded by others. But when thou is spoken, there is no thing. *Thou* has no bounds.

In my elaboration of *unvavish'd* I have not accounted for the *thou*, for its harnessing of the weird magic of invocation, the way it summons the urn's presence onto the page, makes it livingly, almost, appear.

Reading in this January light I am astonished by the pleasure of receptivity. That it is possible to make, out of mere looking, a hollow space for reception, that one's mind can follow, in this way, the traces of another's mind, speak these traces silently to and in oneself and let them take shape again in one's own mind, in one's own body. That you, too, can perform, are performing, this magic. I am astonished by the collapse of time in this activity or indolence: I exist only in the time of this making, this remaking. This thought occupies me as a series of bright waves.

In her writings on "The Self," Weil explicates the relationship between annihilation by external force and the self-annihilation that for her was at the center of religious devotion: "Nothing in the world can rob us of the power to say 'I'. Nothing except extreme affliction. Nothing is worse that an extreme affliction which destroys the 'I' from outside, because after that we can no longer destroy it ourselves."

According to this view, the worst thing about "extreme affliction" is that by turning a self into a thing, it robs that self of the opportunity for deliberate spiritual self-effacement.

If we focus only on the scene of annihilation, can these two processes be distinguished? Is a person who has experienced "extreme affliction" (how extreme?) doomed to confuse violence with salvation?

Thou word-inhabited mind, thou segmented light, thou crust of snow.

The front of Apollo's marble body is draped in a marble cloth that encircles the air behind him, lifted by the wind as he runs. Behind Daphne's marble knee, marble laurel leaves climb between the marble bodies, lifting even into the shadows beneath the marble folds of the drapery. Daphne's marble fingers sprout marble leaves. As if the stone were liquid, were air: everything is in motion; everything touches everything. His arm curves around her. His rand rests where the rising bark meets her vanishing body.

Some numbness attends this attempt. This trying to hold (together) the force of *ravish* and the force of *thou* in the word *desire* (in the world desire). If to say *thou* represents an acceptance of the possibility of the other's refusal—that inside the other is some inaccessible interiority which, wholly apart from us, may say yes or no to us, holds our fate, in this way, in its hands—desire itself may become (why this equivocation and passivity? why this abstraction?) a force that wishes to annihilate. Some numbness attends this attempt. Attend.

That otherness inside her. Some numbness. Some unimagined not-yet. Some unspoken. Some *thou*.

TONIC 4 (Thoreau)

> *I must confess there is nothing so strange to me as my own body. I love any other piece of nature, almost, better.* —Thoreau, *Journal*

For instance this moss overtaking

        the blackened stump the

wood pulling away from the bark a

        crack the depth of which you can't

gauge mosquitos slow and killable

        this late hour of summer in which you feel

the slow dissolve of the social self

        the grooved body of the oak

this picture-feeling of a pleasure you

        wouldn't call *pleasure* some

seasonal drift or weather-being in which

        personhood is no

question

EONEONEONEONEONEONEONEONEONEON
EONEONEONEONEONEONEONEONEONEON
EONEONEONEONEONEONEONEONEONEON
EONEONEONEONEONEONEONEONEONEON
EONEONEONEONEONEONEONEONEONEON
EONEONEONEONEONEONEONEONEONEON
EONEONEONEONEONEONEONEONEONEON
EONEONEONEONEONEONEONEONEONEON
EONEONEONEONEONEONEONEONEONEON
EONEONEONEONEONEONEONEONEONEON
EONEONEONEONEONEONEONEONEONEON
EONEONEONEONEONEONEONEONEONEON
EONEONEONEONEONEONEONEONEONEON
EONEONEONEONEONEONEONEONEONEON

SIX VARIATIONS ON BEETHOVEN'S OPUS 109

A:

The little black squares with which I am typing this sentence are really only the ghosts of keys, closer to the touchscreen of a phone than to the keys of a typewriter, whose fleet and spidery limbs vaulted at the little bracketed-off square of the page, sticking to each other sometimes, in their animal way. The marks were darker if you pressed harder. I read somewhere that the first typewriter was called a "literary piano."

The distance that the small squares beneath my fingers move when I depress the keys is called their "travel," n., as in this review of the 2015 MacBook: "there's very little clack as you type, and only the slightest *travel*." I like this way of describing a spatial difference as a kind of immediately sensible quality. *Travel* and *clack* are ways of reassuring my body that something real is happening when I touch the keys, a reassurance it craves in the face of design's inexorable progress toward the final flatness, like the old story about abstraction in painting. Designers compensate for the lack of travel that has resulted from the drive to flatten by adjusting the "snap ratio," the amount of force required to make each key "fire." The *Popular Mechanics* article I read on this subject instructs me to "press a key slowly and feel out its inertia before it suddenly gives way."

As a percussive instrument, the piano cannot produce a true *legato*, or continuity of sound across the playing of its discrete keys. In this way, the "literary piano" analogy is apt: no matter how close one letter gets to another, margins remain. The composer's note for the A theme indicates that the pianist should make the music "cantabile"—singable or singing, like a voice or a violin. Not, in other words, like a piano.

The delicate machine in my grandmother's perfume-scented spare bedroom produced strings of letters in an elegant cursive. I liked to type the letters with spaces between them because they looked so ghostly that way, each letter holding its trailing arms out to the void. And then when you typed the words close together you could see where the ends met up, or rather where they didn't quite.

I like the letters best that have the little enclosed spaces typographers call *counters*—the oblong hollow of the o, the half-moon of the e—and second best those that have *apertures*, or partially enclosed spaces, like c or n. The lowercase e, counter atop aperture, is my favorite. The counter in a lowercase e is called an eye.

B:

Bladder wrack is a seaweed common along the coast of Maine and distinguished by its vesicles, little pockets of air like distributed lungs which allow it to float on the surface of the sea, maximizing its exposure to the sun. It is anchored to the sand by a holdfast. You imagine the counters in the a and the e of the word *imagine* as vesicles, strung together by a growing thing. Dried, the vesicles become flattened discs, and the fronds become black and brittle.

You ask your pianist friend to explain what makes the series of grace notes followed by a dotted quarter C in the penultimate measure of B theme so beautiful. He offers several plausible sounding explanations, none of which you fully understand.

Wikipedia: *A* holdfast *is a root-like structure that anchors aquatic sessile organisms, such as seaweed, other sessile algae, stalked crinoids, benthic cnidarians, and sponges, to the substrate.*

Lying on the rock looking out at the green sea you count the counters in *vesicle*, *sessile*, and *holdfast*. You haven't said anything about violence yet. The cold of the body in its sudden solitude.

1.

Your pianist friend explains that a grace note is *untimed*, that it has *no rhythmic accountability*. It is smaller than the note it accompanies and decked with little flags.

> Inertia is *a tendency to do nothing or remain unchanged*. I like the second meaning for its suggestion of a kind of modest integrity. At the bottom of your breath you can feel this place in yourself: the edge of your inertia. This is the place where your being would fold, give way, unbecome.

You sometimes feel or imagine that you feel another person's interior weather. Everything you read confirms that this is both a mistake and not a mistake.

> The word violence comes from Latin, meaning *vehemence* or *impetuosity*, words that describe the violent actor. But the online etymological dictionary I consulted also suggests that the word is "probably related to *violare* (see *violation*)," which speaks to the violated object rather than the vehement subject. The question of whether violence is measured by the intention of the subject or by the perception of the object is a slippery one, even here. Its vehemence or violation involves the edge of inertia and what happens when we meet there.

A grace note is *not subject to the time signature*, your friend says. *You just have to fit it in*. The internet adds the words "extra" "not essential" and "embellishment."

> I imagine the grace of the grace note relates to its theological meaning: a free gift, unearned, outside all economies of earning and reward.

The principal note that begins the first variation of the third movement—a B, hovering in the score above the treble clef—is the highest note in the movement to that point. As the third movement unfolds, Beethoven will move the pianist's hands further toward the extremes of the keyboard. Between the grace note (also a B, an octave lower) and the principle, an unspecified duration.

Listening, you always imagine something being broken in this interval. And something being released.

Consider the freedom of extraneous being.

2.

Beethoven's biographer writes: *the sonata as a whole is also informed by the motivic interval of a third*. This means that the pattern or meaning the listener discerns has to do with a particular distance, a discrete span of unplayed notes, repeated in time and space.

> In the second variation, Beethoven includes rests in the left hand when the right hand plays notes of equal duration, and vice versa. The rests have two small flags, indicating that their unsounding should last the duration of a sixteenth note. The alternation between sound and silence, presence and absence, gives this part of the score a kind of symmetry. I can't read music and so can't hear the notes when I see them on the page, but I can see the span of each silence and the non-silence that accompanies it.
>
> *Vesicle, sessile, holdfast*. A mistake and not a mistake. I don't know anything about harmonic intervals but I imagine that I can feel the rightness of this distance the same way I perceive the travel of the keys, the rightness in the spaces between the sounds, the

invisible proportions that make my fingers feel like they are making something happen.

An illness overtakes your time. The illness is characterized by rendering it difficult for sufferers to breathe.

The distance between your body and the world's will that one might call its *inertia* or *integrity* has, you suspect, been eroded, resulting in a gradual reduction in your snap ratio.

Limp and overlapping blades of bladderwrack rise from the rocks to float on the incoming tide. The little waves are lit. You dive under the green surface for a breathless interval. Blank and salt, sunlit and cold. A swarm of small waves. A gull unfolds itself in the whole sky. You don't mind swimming through it, now that you know about its little lungs.

You drove to the movie theater in his pick-up truck. In the movie John Travolta played an angel. On the way back to camp the sky was full of stars and a you swerved for a black bear cub in the road. At the dance, you were aware of him watching but thought you were imagining it. He was engaged, which was impossible and romantic. You remember the female lead tending someone's wounds but it may have been a different film. After the dance, he called you an exhibitionist. Looking through the old camp photos, he said you were the prettiest girl. This felt incorrect because you were very young in the pictures but also exciting to be the prettiest.

Sessility is the biological property of an organism describing its lack of a means of self-locomotion.

I had many opportunities to leave but did not.

You vaguely felt that the engagement must have a tragic dimension.

3.

One result of the sickness is that everyone must separate. This creates additional spaces between things.

Vesicle, sessile, holdfast.

You watch the ongoingness of wave pattern in the counters between spruce limbs. Your son asks, *how many voices do you hear in your head?* You say you don't know. He says *I hear two.*

Three counters and an aperture in *head*: an especially buoyant word.

You had wanted something romantic to happen. Years before, he had presented you with an award at the end-of-summer banquet, a necklace with an engraved silver pendant: *G.O.O.D. Award, 1990.* You fell asleep holding it. When you went swimming at night your friend was often there also, so you were only half surprised about what she told you later in the summer. G.O.O.D. stood for *Great Out of Doors*. You can't remember anything that happened inside his cabin except the strange immobility of your body and his words, none of which clearly indicated any intent to harm.

In the third variation, the left hand answers the right hand in a sort of call and response.

Vesicle, sessile, holdfast.

Not enough inertia, or too much. Everyone uses the same phrase: "floating outside your body." You count the counters in this phrase, imagine it lifted on a green tide and

floating outside my body.

4.

After talking to your pianist friend, you make notes in your notebook. *Harmonic interval: a distance in pitch only. Melodic interval: a distance in pitch and time.*

Everyone misses ordinary contact, being close to other people breathing.

The fourth variation is an extended (impossible) legato. The music strains toward the uninterrupted continuity between notes that it can never achieve.

> I search through more images of cursive typewriter fonts and zoom in to see the little spaces.

You'd lost the necklace in the river the following summer and cried for hours. He said, *You make me feel like I'm seventeen*. You wondered what he meant by *you*. Later you would go to the rope swing at night with only your friend and just drank beer and looked at the stars, no swimming. He found out you knew about each other and wrote you identical notes spelling *truly* with an e in both.

> In retrospect, I like that this misspelling introduces a counter into *truth*, which otherwise has one only in its adjectival form, *true*.

Once at a meditation retreat it occurred to you that what is most terrible about violence is that it is a kind of touching, that the unstated corollary to *everything is interconnected* is that anyone can hurt anyone else at any time. Still, you liked being there, everyone breathing together in the empty space.

5.

In the breaking open between the grace note and its principle, a starry interior or a room of shards.

This cold that enters your body. How bruises find themselves. You didn't. After this a certain signal or architechtonic idea. Being small you played it. Childlike, unbodied, theoretical, you made the coffee. It wasn't something you.

Having retreated from the idea of shared weather, you burrow into a language. Non-being shines whitely at the edges of everything.

The fifth variation, your pianist friend tells you, is contrapuntal, containing *two or more musical lines which are harmonically interdependent yet independent.* At various places in the score, you can see the right hand and the left hand approaching one another and separating again in symmetrical ascending and descending scales, as though compelled toward contact but also fearful.

> Dried bladder wrack inks illegible sentences on the sand. I wonder if our non-sessility doesn't just mean that no holdfast anchors us to the substrate.

Some of our distributed lungs have stopped working. This has to do with who we are and

> how we touch one another.

6.

The composer, who cannot hear the notes he is writing, often composes at the piano. He can see the intervals between his fingers, between his two hands. The sounds produce themselves inside him.

In the sixth and final variation of the third movement, Beethoven increases the frequency of notes per beat, moving from quarter notes to trill and back again. The trill is played by the thumb and index fingers of both hands, while the other fingers play the melody.

A person has imagined this constellation of movements and sounds. A person has left elaborate and precise written instructions for these movements and sounds to be produced by other bodies.

Toward the end of the variation, the trill migrates from the left to the right hand. The small finger of the right hand plays the notes of the theme at the top of the keyboard. My pianist friend calls this *Beethoven's starry firmament*. You imagine the sky above the lake, broken

open.

The sounds produce themselves.

I wonder what I mean by *you*.

NIGHT SEA

What seem at first to be lines are in fact small gaps. A numbing and numberless repetition, waves on a long horizon, diffused light, layers of blue. Minute traces of gold leaf in the worked surface.

The color that predominates is *ultramarine*—beyond the sea—which in the Renaissance was so rare and costly that it was usually used only for the clothing of the virgin Mary.

Consider the relation between spiritual exaltation and expensive elements.

Chantecaille Nano Gold Energizing Rye Cream ($265, nordstrom.com) delivers 24K gold to a cellular level, where its anti-inflammatory benefits can best target eye-related issues like puffiness.

In the early 60s, Martin's work was often dismissed as "decorative."

In the middle of my life I was captured by beauty. In practice, this often resulted in a furtive purchase of expensive objects.

Art historian Suzanne Hudson: *The appearance of gold in Night Sea contributes to its sense of flux. Gold is physically immutable but radically contingent to the effects of atmosphere...It is brute fact and exalted symbol—the siting of gilded surfaces in dark medieval churches, where they served as agents of illumination, reminds us of this.*

The title *Night Sea* may or may not be a reference to the Jungian archetype of the Night Sea Journey, in which the hero is swallowed by a sea monster or descends into an underworld, *a journey to the land of ghosts.*

In the land of ghosts I built a secret life.

Radically contingent to the effects of atmosphere I sought intimate dispersal,
patterned surface, subdivided pane. I asked to be

released

EARLY / OFTEN

> *The paintings are simply attractive, a word which is usually, and is here, used as both a derogation and a compliment.*
> —Donald Judd on Agnes Martin, 1962

The value of your person-object is unpredictably registered and insofar as there are objects and there are objects you'd just as soon be an expensive one, but beggars can't be choosers. Hidden inside the figure of want is the figure of need which everyone wants to destroy. What you think about most is the way that value gets inside you: not a price tag but a kind of ontological swallowing. Someone carved your name in on a library desk under the words HOTTEST FRESHMEN GIRLS but someone else crossed you out.

O (After *Hamlet*)

And, like a neutral to his will and matter, / Did nothing. The engine of your interval ranges blank across the hour. Blank along an inkblack importuning. A blankness rising like a little light. Blank blank my heart, blank my will and matter. These breathing clouds. Brightback the bodies of birds black unbecome. Blankly a ghostword moves among enemy sentences. Like a neutral. For example, want. For example, augury and its defiance. For example, any woman.

o

This nothing's more than matter. A pattern of discrete absences or a light snow. Vacancy of what cloudcovered hour. Slow lit these crystalline grasses, this whitelined leaf pile. Attain to a hollowness. Here coldly. Here, let me.

o

What ceremony else? Else this ache at the base of the skull, else this eyestrain. Else a body other to itself, object before its own mind, skull before its own eyes. Mind you this slow fog; mind you its breaking. Elsewhere lichens break onto the old trees. White casements. Chimney smoke. Elsewhere you occupy a season of impenetrable particulars. Summon each sentence tenderness has spoken to you. World-bereft, their little engines still run. Here the ceremony of grammar makes nothing possible.

o

I think nothing, my lord. Still dark among the carsounds, you empty the night's ashes. Ophelia says the only words she can. Here obedience. Here evasion. You build a small fire over the grate while elsewhere the world takes up its forgotten body. O is a picture, not a sound. O empty circle. O hollow hour. How all occasions do inform your ghosted name, dropped into it, so many little sticks.

o

As one incapable of her own distress. Experiment: what would a woman look like emptied of everything, even her own distress? Leaden clouds delimitate a cold pearlescence. Result: dumb echo. Floral concentrate of sex and singing. The stove sounds its invisible expansion behind the amplified nothing of the fire. The wood you carried an hour ago resolves into a fine ash.

o

You are naught, you are naught: I'll mark the play. Ophelia as naught as knot as not.

o

No, no they do but jest, poison in jest. Witness to a performance of madness, she contracts a real one. You rub the creosote from the glass stove door to better watch the burning. This joke kills her. Everything, even the light, fills with a low disgust. To be so readily annihilated. *Observed of all observers.* Stay low, it whispers.

o

Your honesty should admit no discourse to your beauty. You think, *it snows*, which might mean, *the world snows itself*, or perhaps *the weather is becoming snow*, in any case it obscures the early light, admitting discourse to the vulnerability of every kind of body. In this scene, Ophelia's lover suggests a banishment of the body's effects from the body's interior life. Ophelia revisits this instruction offstage. She, too, is haunted. The specter of her dismemberment settles whitely over everything.

o

but to persever / In obstinate condolement Obstinate, my father's body held its living days or hours past the point of seizure. Outside, still back, still black, still black. *Seizure* as in a laying hold by invisible hands. Consider writing as temporal measure whose unit is a letter. O hands, you make a pile of time. O time. What nothing seizes me? What obstinance? Now a dull light shows the shapes of all the objects that withstood the dark hours. Notwithstanding nothing. O little pile, o occupant. O o o. *Who's there?*

o

And nothing is at a like goodness still This darkness which is not absence but a low hovering concentrate, thick with dark, thick as any January tenor, doubled down in its own too much.

o

all those his lands / Which he stood seized of All those the little snowfall now everywhere unbecomes. All those which may be seized, are seized, are the seizure of the body of the land. In the middle of the sentence, the lichens break into the dawnlight, the body breaks into its beauty. How you may forfeit your own mind, may stand seized of it, by poison or by illness or by any man, by words. Obstinately the little snow.

TONIC 5 (Sonnet)

I LONG TO BE WITH YOU IN ANY OPEN SPACE
I LONG TO BE WITH YOU IN ANY OPEN SPACE
I LONG TO BE WITH YOU IN ANY OPEN SPACE
I LONG TO BE WITH YOU IN ANY OPEN SPACE
I LONG TO BE WITH YOU IN ANY OPEN SPACE
I LONG TO BE WITH YOU IN ANY OPEN SPACE
I LONG TO BE WITH YOU IN ANY OPEN SPACE
I LONG TO BE WITH YOU IN ANY OPEN SPACE
I LONG TO BE WITH YOU IN ANY OPEN SPACE
I LONG TO BE WITH YOU IN ANY OPEN SPACE
I LONG TO BE WITH YOU IN ANY OPEN SPACE
I LONG TO BE WITH YOU IN ANY OPEN SPACE
I LONG TO BE WITH YOU IN ANY OPEN SPACE
I LONG TO BE WITH YOU IN ANY OPEN SPACE

LATE SPRING

Against the white the dark-light body of the lilac, bark stripped in places, the branches curve the way a thing twisted will curve. There are the minutes, there is the white between the branches of the lilac. To begin a sentence with *there is* or *there are* is to commit a style error known as a *dummy subject* which is something like a driverless car, though I prefer to think of it as a ship piloted by a ghost. I only recently noticed the continual sensation, running like little rivulets of snowmelt alongside or under the years, of my own meagerness.

Late March still light the fire. Little licks all light the dark kitchen. Even the first breaths hurt this hurt, all inward, all interior. You are bored of it. Collaborator, you inward utter. A million little fibers extending before a thought crosses. What mirrored blank you will yourself, what naught. Grayblue the dull morning. Picture a self all surface, picture a picture.

Snow articulates the trees, each its own in the whited stillness. Sometimes you are inhabited by hollowness, the thought-feeling of emptiness which is itself empty, clear-filigreed edge of dark ice around dark water. And then you are cold all over, remembering your body in postures of abjection. Only a small creek, unowned. You may have it for your metaphor. *For this relief much thanks.* Something monstrous in all this making: matter swirling around anti-matter, paraphernalia of nothing.

ARKS OF REPRIEVE

What was offered: oak leaf, spider web, dried leaves in a white bowl

What we took: hours, language, proximity

RITUAL

Sometimes you are
inhabited by hollowness, the
thought-feeling of emptiness which
is itself empty, clear-filigreed edge
of dark ice around dark water.

And then you are cold all over,
remembering.

EONEONEONEONEONEONEONEONEONEON
EONEONEONEONEONEONEONEONEONEON
EONEONEONEONEONEONEONEONEONEON
EONEONEONEONEONEONEONEONEONEON
EONEONEONEONEONEONEONEONEONEON
EONEONEONEONEONEONEONEONEONEON
EONEONEONEONEONEONEONEONEONEON
EONEONEONEONEONEONEONEONEONEON
EONEONEONEONEONEONEONEONEONEON
EONEONEONEONEONEON   EONEONEON
EONEONEONEONEONEONEONEONEONEON
EONEONEONEONEONEONEONEONEONEON
EONEONEONEONEONEONEONEONEONEON
EONEONEONEONEONEONEONEONEONEON

THE INVISIBLE COUNTRY OF REMADE DESIRE

In the invisible country of remade

        desire there is no anthem or flag only a letter in

a worn envelope passed between citizens;

        this gesture is at once a

declaration of statehood and the cross-

        ing of its borders.

In this state there is no

        eye cream with or without

24K gold. The letter is written on

        onionskin in faded ink, typed

on mimeograph paper, minutely sealed

        in a miniature envelope, scratched

onto a leaf. It says

        I long to be with you

                        in any open space.

NOTES

DAPHNE, pp. 5-16

Hugh Parry, "Ovid's Metamorphoses: Violence in the Pastoral Landscape," *Transactions and Proceedings of the American Philological Association*, 95:268-282, 1964; Suzan Campbell, "Interview with Agnes Martin," May 15, 1989, transcript, Archive of American Art, Smithsonian Institution, Washington DC. 10-11, Francine Russo, "Sexual Assault May Trigger Involuntary Paralysis," *Scientific American* online, https://www.scientificamerican.com/article/sexual-assault-may-triggerinvoluntary-paralysis/; "Apparent Death," *Wikipedia;* https://en.wikipedia.org/wiki/Apparent_death; "Tonic," *New Oxford American Dictionary*; "Laurel," *Wikipedia* https://en.wikipedia.org/wiki/Laurus_nobilis; "Ravish," *New Oxford American Dictionary.*

ON CERTAINTY, pp. 18-39

William Shakespeare, Sonnet 116; Rosemarie Waldrop, *Curves to the Apple*; Ludwig Wittgenstein, *Philosophical Investigations*; Ludwig Wittgenstein, *On Certainty*; Ray Monk, *Ludwig Wittgenstein: The Duty of Genius.*

HORROR VACUI, pp. 41-47

Simone Weil, "The Iliad: Or, The Poem of Force"; "Plato's Timaeus," *The Stanford Encyclopedia of Philosophy*; "Parmenides," *The Stanford Encyclopedia of Philosophy*; Peter Adamnson, "A Brief History of Nothing" (YouTube); Andrew Marvell, "The Garden,"; Louis Menand, "The Women Come and Go," *The New Yorker*, September 30, 2002.

UNRAVISH'D, pp. 49-62

John Keats, "Ode on a Grecian Urn"; Dan Beachy-Quick, *A Brighter Word Than Bright: Keats at Work*; Simone Weil, *The Iliad, or The Poem of Force*; Martin Buber, *I and Thou.*

NIGHT SEA, pp. 74-75

Nordstrom.com; Suzanne Hudson, *Agnes Martin: Night Sea* (Afterall Books 2017).

O, pp. 77-79

William Shakespeare, *Hamlet.*

TONIC 5 (Sonnet) p. 80

From a letter from Francis Skinner to Ludwig Wittgenstein, April 4, 1934.

LATE SPRING, p. 81

William Shakespeare, *Hamlet*

ARKS OF REPRIEVE, p. 82

Title phrase taken from Emily Dickinson 1506

THE INVISIBLE COUNTRY OF REMADE DESIRE, p. 85

Italicized text from a letter from Francis Skinner to Ludwig Wittgenstein, April 4, 1934.